Robert Bird

Law Lyrics

Robert Bird

Law Lyrics

ISBN/EAN: 9783744775991

Printed in Europe, USA, Canada, Australia, Japan

Cover: Foto ©Thomas Meinert / pixelio.de

More available books at **www.hansebooks.com**

LAW LYRICS

GLASGOW

WILSON & McCORMICK, Saint Vincent Street

1885

TO

My Brethren of the Long Robe

THESE LYRICS ARE DEDICATED

WITH A HOPE THAT THEY MAY BE FOUND

NOT LESS

CHEERFUL IN SESSION

THAN

CHARMING IN VACATION

BY

THE AUTHOR

CONTENTS.

FIRST LINES.

LAW LYRICS.

SPRING IN COURT.

SPEAK not to me of budding boughs,
  Of leafy hedges, greeny mazes,
Of ivied banks and primrose walks,
  Of pastures spotted white with daisies:
  My bardic ire it only raises
To think of Nature at her sport
  While men are fog-lost in the hazes
Of dingy case in dungeon court.

Oh! why has sage Professor Bell
  From his good Principles left out
The law that makes man greet the Spring
  With universal song and shout?
  What Act instructs the feathered rout
To mate, or take their annual trip?
  Good lack! the point is left in doubt
By even Clark on Partnership!

I fear our Erskines, Stairs, and Humes
    Have only learnt the world by half ;
And that there must be wider laws
    Unjacketed by sheep or calf :
    But then, 'twould only make you laugh
To hear them sung from legal twig,
    Where, like a bat-winged bag of chaff,
Sits Justice in a foozle-wig.

THE JURYMAN'S CAROL.

It was a warm hairst day,
  A day the farmer grudges,
When I was called away
  To meet the Circuit Judges:
My tie was Holland brown,
  My coat green, I assure ye,
For I had come to town
  To sit upon the jury.

In court, the ballot drawn,
  The jury benched compactly,
Then I was bid begone
  And come at two exactly;
I went, I came, and then
  All time and honour scorning
I was bid come again
  At ten o'clock next morning.

And then began the show—
  We sat on wooden benches,
Sweet fifteen in a row,
  All ravelled in our senses;
While wigs of horse-hair flew
  To questions, speeches, wrangling,
Pulling the cases through,
  Like lassies at a mangling.

A lad or two for theft
  Of handkerchiefs and purses,
A poet who had reft
  His fancy of bad verses;
And many cases more
  Of evil predilections,
With constables who swore
  To previous convictions.

And fast through thick and thin,
  'Mong all their hilty-tilty,
We brought the prisoners in
  Unanimously guilty;
Resolved whate'er the crime,
  In spite of fuss or fizziness,
To save each tick of time
  That kept us from our business.

THE SPARROW.

BROWN-BACKIT, dusty-breasted chappie !
Wi' streakit throat, and pow sae nappy,
Wi' sturdy legs and neb sae rappy
        For fechtin' splore.
Thy cheery chirp mak's a' things happy
        Aboot my door.

In some tree fork, nane thick wi' leaves,
Or darksome hole aneath the eaves,
A harum-scarum nest thou weaves
        O' strings and straws,
That trailin' fast, thou rugs and rieves
        Frae kings or craws.

In simmer's prime, the world's thy ain,
To range the fields and scour the plain;—
O' farmers' guns, fear thou hast nane !
        Or thowless rattles;
But helter-skelter at the grain
        Thou yirps and battles.

When winter comes, thou begs nae pity,
But townward hies, wi' chirping ditty,
Hailing wi' yellochs in the city
        Ilk frien' thou meets,
To win thy bread, and coup the kitty
        In vera streets.

Gi'e finches fine their music mellow,
Gi'e blackbirds trig their nebs o' yellow,
The redbreast, tae—the sodger fellow—
         His sang sae sma';
In clatterin' noisome chorus bellow
            Thou dings them a'.

But haud!   I dinna like thy fechtin',
Whan, breast tae breast, hot war thou'rt wechtin';
Strivin' wi' hangin' wings tae strechtin'
         On yird thy foe ;
Crumbs fa' for a', and nebs fast dichtin',
          Work endless woe !

Kings mak' the wars, and fules tak' swurds,
And cloor ilk ither intae curds ;
But men o' sense, and bonnie birds,
           Wi' brains tae harrow,
Should fecht their battles oot wi' words,
          My wee cock sparrow !

Ance in a riddle-trap I caught thee,
And to a strugglin' captive brought thee ;
But 'twas na dabs or kicks that got thee
         Thy wings sae fleet ;
'Twas thy wee burstin' heart that bought thee
         Thy freedom sweet.

Black shame to the unworthy son
Wad lift on thee a murderous gun,
And through thy ranks, as thou dost run,
            Pour spreading lead,
To see thee fall, with wings undone,
            And bleeding head.

Nae gun hae I, or dog, or warden ;
Thou'rt welcome to my house and garden ;
I dinna heed thy thefts ae farden
            Frae simmer tae simmer:
Thou hast my love, my peace, my pardon—-
            Thou blythesome comer.

THE SHERIFF'S FAREWELL TO HIS WIG.

FAREWELL, farewell ! my horsehair wig,
  My snuff-box, tie, and spectacles;
My silken gown, my long goose quills,
  My desk, my ink receptacles ;
Farewell, my handsome high stuffed chair,
  Thou throne of stout invincibles !
For little John has piped the doom
  Of Scotland's Sheriff Principals.

No more officials at my door
  Will bow and say that courts do wait ;
A king without a kingdom is,
  This lordly superannuate.
No more an agent's nose to snub
  When fancy or my humour suits;
No more of humble Sheriff-Clerks,
  Or smiling Sheriff-Substitutes.

No longer avizandum made
  Or foolish notes will shock you, for
My last note soon will echo with
  A final interlocutor.
The feathered shaft is in the string,
  And yet 'twill take ere I am tricked,
A Queen and Parliament to serve
  My last perpetual interdict.

Farewell, my wig ! farewell, my men !
  From Process-clerk to Chancellor,
Ye spirits dark of dusky wing,
  Oh ! ye have much to answer for !
In wax-work soon I may be grouped,
  Or tanked in some aquarium;
But first in humble faith I wait
  My handsome honorarium.

MY OLD GOOSE QUILL.

YE artists, and ye etchers all,
    Of velveteen and plush,
With easels, stools, and stretchers all,
    Chalk, needle, stump, and brush,
I dare your whole utensils fine,
    Your oils and pigment mill,
To match with paints or pencils fine
    My old goose quill.

With birse of independence up,
    Defences he can draw,
And shut a condescendence up
    With stirring pleas in law;
In prayers that thrill in reading of,
    In statement, fact, and will,
Like music is the screeding of
    My old goose quill.

Ye painters have on palette got
    The lark in sunny cloud,
But nowhere in your wallet got
    His song that rings so loud ;
And so you pass completely from
    The ripple and the trill
That chirps and flows so sweetly from
    My old goose quill.

With one ink drop upon it, sirs,
    This plume of barn-fowl's wing,
In summons, or in sonnet, sirs,
    Can make the paper sing ;
And then when love or Latin does
    His liquid bosom thrill,
He runs like any rattan, does
    My old goose quill.

HILL-CLIMBING.

ONCE on a lazy autumn afternoon,
Low-humming to myself an antique tune,
I picked my steps along a Highland path,
That rose steep-winding from the brook-cut strath;
My stout oak staff for climbing, less than resting,
My dog through brackens leaping, grasses breasting
Through bog of peat, through myrtle and red heather,
We climbed, enjoying much the balmy weather,
Till one hill-top my mild desire had crowned,
Then sat I down to view the country round.
Was I alone? Nay, nay! he's ne'er alone,
Who in his mind a merry stage doth own,
Where preach and go, that others may appear,
The mighty masters of the inner ear;
Who never fail to speak a noble part
To him who wears the world upon his heart.

THE TABLE O' FEES.

AIR—" The Laird o' Cockpen."

O, HOW oft hae I heard
  That our whole stock-in-trade
Is a desk for a yaird
  And a pen for a spade—
While it maun be agreed,
  There's a world's guid in these,
Yet oor best pock o' seed
  Is the table o' fees.

For the desk and the stule,
  Wi' a sigh let me say,
May be props for a fule
  At the end of the day,
But like manna and snaw,
  Or a peck o' white peas,
For the doves o' the law
  Is the table o' fees.

Let the merchantman boast
  O' his fine speculations,
And the clergyman hoast
  O'er his teinds' allocations,

For a steady on-cost,
    Banking up the bawbees,
Like a warm dreepin' roast
    Is the table o' fees.

Man! it gangs wi' a clack !
    Like a mill makin' flour;
Three-and-fourpence a crack !
    Six-and-eightpence an hour;
Half-a-crown for a wink,
    And a shillin' a sneeze,
Come like stour o' sma' ink
    Frae the table o' fees.

I could hand ye my stule,
    Ruler, ink-horn, and dask;
I could hand ye my quill,
    Or whate'er ye micht ask;
And could yet wi' my tongue—
    Whilk nae man can appease
Fill a cask tae the bung
    Frae the table o' fees.

THE SHERIFF'S INQUISITION.

SOME sing the songs of Mars,
　And some the lays of Cupid,
In verses clear as stars,
　Or stanzas thick and stupid.
To chant of love or wars
　Will never be my mission,
Till I have sung in bars
　The Sheriff's Inquisition.

There is a little room,
　A trifle close and fusty,
Where legal books illume
　The solemn shelves so dusty;
Where sits a little man,
　'Tis part of whose profession,
To fish out, if he can,
　The prisoner's transgression.

Through his enchanted door
　Each prisoner is guarded;
Once safely on the floor,
　Each chink is watched and warded.
No agent may he see
　For fear he be contamined,
And should collected be
　When sifted and examined.

Of course, he first is told
     He need not aid committal;
But should he silence hold,
     It does not mean acquittal;
For all this little plan,
     This simple institution,
Is not to aid the man,
     But help the prosecution.

If garrulous and weak,
     His words are most nutritious;
Should he refuse to speak,
     'Tis all the more suspicious.
Why not at once up-snap,
     In this age of transition,
This secret chamber trap,
     The Sheriff's Inquisition?

OATMEAL.

WHEN round and red the harvest moon
Keeks wi' bleered ee the trees aboon,
And tasselled corn, wi' nodding croon,
  Stands stiff and strang,
The farmer thinks next day gin noon
  Will find him thrang.

Nae jinkin' teeth, or birlin' wheel,
Shall reap his crap wi' fearsome squeal,
But brawny arms and circling steel
  Will do the wark ;
Where'er he goes wi' hearty zeal
  He'll lea' his mark.

He dichts his scythe, and wi' his stane
Gars ilka side o't ring again,
Till sharpened as 'twad nick a bane
  He wades waist deep,
And half a sheaf o' rustlin' grain
  Fa's wi' ilk sweep.

The ruddy lassies, pleased and thrang,
Bind up the sheaves wi' straw-rape strang,
Whiles liltin' out a rantin' sang
  Ne'er fand in books,
Till a' the field, clean raked alang,
  Stan's reared in stooks.

A week o' dryin' wind and sun,
And out the vera weans maun run,
A' dancin' daft tae get begun
      And dae their parts,
Tae hae a day o' glorious fun
      Amang the carts.

And ere the sun blinks in the wast
The fecht o' forks is ower and past ;
The waving field is hame at last,
      In farmyaird stackit,
The golden treasures, safe and fast,
      Weel raiped and thackit.

When hoary winter nips the air,
Upon the dusty threshing-flair,
The loundering flails mak' music rare
      Wi' thuds and rings ;
While straw flees here, and seeds flee there,
      In heaps and bings.

Then, loaded fu' wi' tentic skill,
The carts gang clinkin' ower the hill
To where the sandstanes bumm their fill
      Like rings o' licht,
And dips the wat wheel o' the mill
      Frae morn tae nicht.

OATMEAL.

And there, aneath the birlin' stane,
The broken corn sheds out like rain,
Tae be shooled plowterin' back again
  And grunded weel,
Till bulgin' pokes hang doon amain
  Wi' painch o' meal.

Oatmeal ! that wanders ower the warl
To smile in ilka housewife's barrel,
Wi' choicest grit for cake, or farl,
  And parritch fine,
That hauds in health the auldest carl
  O' ninety-nine !

Some hae their wealth in land and rock,
And some in ships and some in stock,
And some in bank wi' bolt and lock
  Tae scare the deil,
But my best wealth's in ae wee pock
  That nane wad steal.

THE CHRISTMAS RECESS.

A SONG for the bench and the bar!
   A song for the crown and the vassal!
Mouth stopped is the trumpet of war,
   With mistletoe, laughter, and wassail.
The wig may be hung on the pin,
   The gown may be hooked in like station:
Hail holly! with thee, welcome in
   The joys of the Christmas vacation.

Oh! period of ointments and balms,
   When truce for a season concluding,
Pursued and pursuer take drams,
   And cut up their goose and plum pudding.
Oh! fortnight of frolic and fun,
   When friendship runs wild o'er the nation—
Cards, boxes, cake, shortbread, and bun,
   The gifts of the Christmas vacation!

No longer we'll chop logic roots,
   But sing with broad smiles on our faces,
A dress coat's the best of all suits,
   A hamper the best of all cases.
A fig for the ninny who prates
   Of idlers without occupation ;·
We'll chant with the carols and waits
   The charms of the Christmas vacation.

THE PRISONER'S CRY.

Ye matrons with bright faces and
  Ye men of Britain's clime,
Who think of civil cases, and
  Not criminals or crime ;
While blessings down are fluttered by
  Your bright peculiar star,
Oh, hear the cry that's uttered by
  The prisoner at the bar.

You hear of British justice, and
  Of equity in courts,
From priests in lawn and surplice, and
  That mercy there resorts :
Where judges strip the glory from
  The words of prince, or Czar,
Yet may not sift the story from
  The prisoner at the bar.

Why should the civil suitor be
  A witness for himself,
Though he a rough freebooter be
  For thousand pounds of pelf ;
While for the crimes of pennyworth,
  That make a life or mar,
We do not treat as any worth
  The prisoner at the bar?

Men, innocent, in ages past,
    Have hung, we know full well :
How many, writ in pages past,
    We guess, but cannot tell.
Why longer with old motions, then,
    Arm death's destroying car,
To slay with foolish notions, then,
    The prisoner at the bar ?

He sits, all cowed and quaking there,
    Not one word may he say ;
And hears, with rough heart breaking there,
    His freedom sworn away ;
And witnesses are bidden in
    To speak, from near and far,
While truth itself lies hidden in
    The prisoner at the bar.

THE POOL.

I KNOW a pool, where shadows fall
From fir-trees, melancholy tall,
That dream and quiver round the rim,
And in the molten centre swim,
Where taper tops do all unite
Bemirrored in its silvern light.

At eve, when through the dusky pines
The scarlet of the sunset shines,
There does the blackbird's throat of jet
Pour music soft as flageolet,
That wins an answer, faint and still,
In echoes from the far-off hill.

As gloaming gathers into night
The water-picture loses light,
And, filled with dark reflection's deep,
Seems like a mind perplexed in sleep,
Where spectral thoughts do weave and pass
Behind the surface of the glass.

SEPARATION AND DIVORCE.

THAT justice and right, should be matters of
    money!
  Oh, who could believe it?   What man can endure
That Scotland should harbour—so brave and so
    sunny!—
  A law for the rich and a law for the poor?

A wife for gross cruelty, seeks separation,
  And aliment asks for herself and her chicks:
Pay down fifty pounds, is the way of our nation,
  Or else be content with your blows and your
    kicks!

A man may desire to obtain a divorce
  From crime and unfaithfulness, sorrow and
    pain:
Pay down fifty pounds, is the answer of course,
  Or take your wife back to your bosom again!

The reason is plain: In our high Court of Session
  Such suits must be brought, 'mid a hailstorm of
    fees
For wax and red tape, and—excuse the expression—
  To keep up an Advocates' Guild, if you please.

The cure's with the Sheriff: Give him jurisdiction
 To try all such cases with poverty prest ;
The cost would be small, and at every conviction
 A wrong would be righted, a house would be blest.

Oh, why should Scotch justice be measured by
  purses,
While innocence writhes in an infamous chain?
While children's young ears ring with quarrels and
  curses,
 And women, heart-broken, beg pity in vain.

ON HANGINGS.

LIFE for a life ! life for a life !
  Is bench and pulpit preaching—
But, death by bullet, rope, or knife,
  Is strangely heathen teaching ;
For if to stop a mortal's breath
  Is horrid murder reckoned,
To add to that another death
  Is surely murder second.

What right has man to say to man—
  "A fortnight for contrition,
And then, with all the haste we can,
  We'll launch you to perdition ?"
'Twere better far—it seems to me—
  More Christian and more thorough,
To say that he'd imprisoned be
  To spend his life in sorrow.

If 'tis for punishment on earth,—
  A life in prison spending,
Were sentence of far greater worth,
  Than speeding on life's ending :
And if for punishment in hell,—
  Ere from the clay 'tis riven,
Why with your priests invade the cell,
  To preen a soul for heaven ?

Small chance is there, when all within
  Is surging agitation,
To change a life-long course of sin,
  And work a soul's salvation :
For who the difference fine could trace
  'Tween terror and repentance,
When glowering in death's grizzly face
  Beneath a hanging sentence ?

I speak not of the widespread harm
  Called "warning the defaulters,"
Of swinging men at gallows' arm,
  Like soulless brutes in halters ;
The dreadful drop, the hooded head—
  The same for man or woman !—
Were fitter for a nation bred
  In savagery inhuman.

That guiltless men have died, we know,
  Our hanging system under ;
And why we still a-hanging go,
  Is matter for much wonder :
'Twere better that ten guilty wights
  Should 'scape, remorse to cherish,
Than that, beneath the hangman's rites,
  One innocent should perish.

The hand that gave the vital spark,
   'Tis His alone should quench it ;
No other power should stab the mark,
   Or from its socket wrench it.
A human law, by wit of man,
   Is but a law infernal—
If in its small terrestrial plan
   It clashes with th' eternal.

UP THE DIM GLEN.

HUSHED were the songs of eve, the thrush
    Had hymned the last cloud's roseate lining,
The star of love, with growing blush,
    On night's warm breast lay softly shining;
The air was balmed with meadow-sweet,
    Like arrows shot the burn's clear water,
As on the bridge, with restless feet,
    Dick waited for the miller's daughter.

The moon that chambered in the cloud,
    Looked forth with cheerful roguish greeting
When, on his heart with throbbings loud,
    The old clock struck the hour of meeting.
A red glow filled her father's door,
    A graceful, gliding form revealing,
And soon, with welcomes o'er and o'er,
    Dick met her, through the long grass stealing.

Up the dim glen they took their way,
    With love untold between them beating,
A witness soon was each green spray
    To vows, that here need no repeating.
As homeward slow their steps they bent,
    Her heart was full, her cheeks were burning,
For hands, kept single as they went,
    Were fondly locked on their returning.

HOW WE GO COURTING.

In coat of inky black
  Of worn and sad expression,
We bear upon our back
  The tale of our profession :
A-courting all we go,
  A process each arm under too !
In winter through the snow,
  Through hail and rain, and thunder too!

The music of the bar
  Upon the legal fiddle,
Heard faintly from afar,
  Sounds much like fol-de-riddle;
But once within the door,
  Where everything in fitness is,
In twos upon the floor
  We reel the swearing witnesses.

And if the suit be won,
  With mental frisk and frolic,
We watch the vanquished Hun,
  Convulsed with legal colic;
But should the fight be lost,
  Like Homer's gods, confounding all,
We vanish with a hoast,
  And clay-pipe clouds surrounding all.

True Quixotes of the pen,
  We charge with visage solemn
All sheep that look like men
  Down column after column;
But then we ne'er allow
  A love that's lost to fetter one,
For, with a courtly bow,
  We turn to win a better one.

SCOTCH PORRIDGE.

OWER Scotland's corn the laverocks whustle,
Amang the rigs the corncraiks rustle,
Frae gowden taps the millstanes jostle
          And heap wi' health,
Auld Scotland's cog of grit, and gristle—
          A nation's wealth.

Ye wha wad ken life's pleasures sweet,
Wad haud the doctor in the street,
Wad mak' the tichtest twa en's meet
          Whan scant o' siller,
Taste parritch fine ! and thy glad feet
          Will chase the miller.

In boilin' water, salted weel,
'Tween fingers, rin the ruchsome meal,
While the brisk spurtle gars them wheel
          In jaups an' rings—
Ae guid half-hour, syne bowls may reel
          Wi' food for kings.

Nae butter, syrups, sugar brown,
For him wha sups shall creesh thy crown,
But milk alane, maun isle thee roun',
          Till thou dost soom,
Then a' he needs is ae lang spoon,
          And elbow room.

Gie France her puddocks and ragous,
Gie England puddings, beef, and stews,
Gie Ireland taties, shamrocks, soos,
        And land sae bogie,
True Scotchmen, still will scaud their mou's
        Ower Scotland's cogie.

Puir parritch! here thou'rt scant respeckit,
For frizzled fare, thou'rt aft negleckit;
But Grecian Sparta sune was wreckit
        'Mang drinkin' horns,
And Scotia's thristle may be sneckit
        When thee she scorns.

But, mark the Scot ayont the sea
Welcome his meal, wi' dewy e'e,
He gars the first made parritch flee
        Frae out the dish,
While, that his pock neer toom may be,
        Is a' his wish.

Proud Scotland's sons, o' hill and glen,
Ha'e roused the world frae en' tae en'
Wi' doughty deeds o' tongue and pen,
        And dauntless steel –
Oh, what has made these mighty men
        But Scotland's meal?

On Bannockburn, and freedom's day,
When Britons met in war's array,
E'en though the Northmen knelt to say
　　　　Their creed or carritch,
What made some differ in that fray
　　　　Was Scotland's parritch.

For makin' flesh and buildin' banes,
There ne'er was siccan food for weans,
It knits their muscles steeve as stanes,
　　　　And teuch as brasses;
Fills hooses fu' o' boys wi' brains,
　　　　And rosy lassies.

My blessing on the dusty miller!
Wha gi'es me gowden health for siller!
My blessing on each honest tiller,
　　　　Wha breaks the clod,
And gars green corn, Death's foe and killer,
　　　　Spring frae the sod.

MY LIBRARY.

GREAT spirits of the legal dead !
  Who never smile nor laugh,
With ribs of paper, glue and thread,
  And winding sheets of calf ;
That fame is writ in sand, we're told,
  And shifts with tides and weather;
Then what of names in flaming gold !
  And titles writ in leather ?

In volumes from the Session guns,
  That split the fogs of Court,
My ears, the breath of battle stuns,
  With loud and long report:
Of wigs at sea and men at law,
  Brave Kettie trumps the glory;
While Morrison, Dunlop, and Shaw,
  Prolong the inky Story.

Some curious things I never fail
  To find, my shelves among,
A Stair, with neither steps nor rail,
  A Bell without a tongue;
An Abbot that no priesthood fills,
  A Dove that scares freebooters;
Rob Thomson's bills, Maclaren's wills,
  And forms of Courtly Soutar's.

I have no time for further fumes
  Regarding such fine persons
As Erskines, Frasers, Dicksons, Humes,
  M'Glashans, and M'Phersons.
But take the word of one who smacks
  His thigh, as teeth he gnashes;
Let golden calves be on their backs,
  Their insides are but ashes.

THE LANDLORD'S HYPOTHEC.

THERE was a small grocer
  Who took a small shop,
But soon, you must know, sir,
  He came to a stop;
He found, to his sorrow,
  No cash in his till,
And none could he borrow
  On bond or on bill.

As red as a rocket
  The landlord came down,
And said he must stock it,
  By law of the Crown;
And then upon credit
  He purchased some jams,
And deep went in debit
  For cheeses and hams.

Without hesitation
  The laird for his rent
Laid on Sequestration,
  With double intent:
For six months to go, sir,
  And six in the past,
Until the small grocer
  Was bankrupt at last

With bidding, and knocking,
　　A bold auctioneer,
Sold fittings, and stocking
　　The landlord to clear;
And then the small shoppie
　　Was boarded—" To Let,"
And so the wee trappie
　　Was baited and set.

The laird got the money,
　　While creditors small—
For hams, cheese, and honey
　　Got nothing at all:
They cried—" Whirlietoddy !
　　This never can be ! "
And all in a body
　　Came trooping to me.

They smote on their pockets,
　　And wanted to know !
How to the red rocket's
　　Their money should go ?
But Pagans and Gothics
　　Should all understand—
The landlord's hypothec 's
　　The law of the land !

THE POOR AGENT.

YE men who roll in carriages
  And swim in coppered yachts,
Who make your wealthy marriages
  And think your easy thoughts,
Of all the sights you wink upon,
  That shock you and allure,
Pray, do you ever think upon
  The Agent of the Poor?

Within our legal coterie,
  In May-time of the year,
We, from a lawyer's lottery,
  Draw sixteen by the ear;
The sight a pretty pageant is,
  But irksome to endure,
For oft the poorest agent is
  The Agent of the Poor.

The poor of every parish have
  Their doctor, at the least;
Workhouses, Scotch and Irish, have
  Their clergyman or priest;
Each guardian of the pauper, gets
  His salary made sure,
But not one single copper gets
  The Agent of the Poor.

We hear so much of charity
　　In public now-a-days,
'Twere surely small vulgarity
　　To tell our simple ways.
The merchant prince so gallant, spends
　　His guinea on the cure ;
His purse, his time, his talent lends
　　The Agent of the Poor.

A STILL LAKE.

DUSK, as an oval shield of beaten steel,
The still lake lies: its level waters feel
The autumn of the bright long laboured year-
The bliss of rest.   Suspended dream-like, clear,
In its calm tide, the circling kingdom swims.
The silver shore that girds its waveless rims,
Steals unperceived into the glassy deep:
And castellated rocks where birches weep,
Where hazels droop, crowned by the rowan bold,
O'er-frost the flood with scarlet and leaf-gold:
While, flowing down the verging trees between,
Dyed is the wave with streaks of grassy green.
Caught from a sloping square of stubble field,
The rising hills their patch of yellow yield,
And heather holms, and reach of bracken lands
Blush in the flood, and bathe their russet hands,
While at the further end, with shoulder high
A purple mountain pushes out the sky—
That gentle sky! of blue and pearly flake
That fills with heav'n the whole remaining lake.

And so the mirror's held to nature.   Thus
On thought's clear glass, like scenes may shine
    on us.

D

But let a squall smite on the steely blue,
Then not one trembling image will be true,
And should the breeze outspread his blurring
    wings
The whole suspended world will fade in rings,
And yet, should calm once more regain its sway
The glass will smile again with scenery gay.

IN PRAISE OF INK.

Of all the drops in bottles corked,
  Of stoneware, glass, or wicker,
There's not a fluid that excels
  Black ink—celestial liquor!
With thee I slake my thirsty pen,
  And make him sing and whistle;
For Erin's shamrock, England's rose,
  And Scotland's ragged thistle.

Take black ink for the virgin draft,
  And scarlet to revise it,
Take purple for a hindmost touch,
  And blue to emphasize it ;
Of all the various stoppered streams,
  Then yield the laurels triple
To mildly flowing blue-black ink,
  Thou prince of lawyers' tipple!

With thee the scribe on sheepskin drums
  Makes music sweet as Ariel ;
Tunes inharmonious title deeds
  With instruments notarial.
When minor into major glides,
  He marks the change symphonial
With proving tenor's bass infeft,
  And duet matrimonial.

I've heard of bards who thought to climb
   Parnassus by hard drinking,
And seemed on Pegasus to soar
   While pewter pots kept clinking;
But some can rise beyond the skies
   Without one drunken caper;
Astride a quill well charged with ink,
   And winged with sheets of paper.

Let painters keep their colours fine,
   Their brushes, pots, and pigments—
I know of sheens and shines and hues
   That scorn such oily figments;
A feathered shaft and ebon bead
   Can net the moonbeam slender,
And flood old Scotland's lochs and glens
   With sheets of golden splendour.

THE RIVER BAILIE.

FAIR Clyde! whose waters wimpling trot
By hawthorn bow'r and rose-hung cot.
To wash the star Forget-me-not
   From daisied sod,
Hast thou forgotten thou hast got
   A river god?

From scutcheoned coach to court he flits,
His small Neptunian brow he knits,
And leaving law to lesser wits
   Of legal clod,
A law unto himself he sits,
   This river-god.

Red lightnings clothe his Jove-like chair
With curtains deep and yards to spare,
While buttoned angels hover there,
   Deep blue and broad,
Who greet with low obsequious air
   The river-god.

He hears a clash of seamen's tales,
Of starboard bows and weather rails,
Till, fankled up in ropes and sails,
   With azure nod,
He dreams of butter, cheese, and scales
   This river-god.

He wakes and, with Olympian snort,
Finds starboard clashing still with port;
With law so long and life so short,
        He shakes his rod,
Fines all for being in his court,
        The river-god.

Oh, sunny waves of crystal beam,
Uplift the genius of thy stream,
With ireful trident raised supreme
        And red barbed shod,
Hurl headlong hence from useless dream
        This river-god!

LOVELY DELIA.

WILDLY! wildly beats the heart,
　　That is caught in Cupid's chains,
Thrilled with every wayward dart,
　　Harbinger of lover's pains;
Beating low and throbbing high,
　　Moving down love's dizzy dance,
Melted by a liquid eye,
　　Frozen by an icy glance.

Saddest far beneath the sky
　　Is the face thou soon must leave:
Fairest fair to memory's eye
　　Lives the form of yester-eve;
Lovely Delia thou wilt find
　　Lovelier grows when forced to part,
Flaming in the absent mind,
　　Fuelled by the faithful heart.

THE SHERIFF-SUBSTITUTE'S LAMENT.

THE summer sun flames hotly through
  My window squares of dustiness,
And seeks in vain with golden dew
  To melt my mental crustiness.
The wheels of court are locked in cog,
  Without one plea to mitigate ;
There's not a man, or ass, or dog,
  Has courage left to litigate.

The country's done! My calf-bound books
  Nod all their backs in weariness,
One dusty red-taped process looks
  From pigeon holes of eerieness.
I've got no work to do ; I yawn
  For cats for my Kilkennydom,
And sometimes think the peaceful dawn
  Breaks of the great millennium.

When court day comes, my wig and stole
  I scarce can don for laziness ;
The crier cries his morning roll
  And weeps for tabling business.
My mind has reached a weary state
  Beyond the prick of raillery,
With leaving early, coming late,
  And calling for my salary.

Perchance upon the banks of Nith,
  When comes the long vacationing,
I'll find my spirits rising with
  Good weather and good rationing ;
Or wading in some dusky burn,
  With basket, rod, and leafy roof,
I'll thank the autumn stars that turn
  My silken gown to waterproof.

THE SHERIFF AND THE COW.

BE-NECKTIED, be-wigged, and be-gowned,
  Be-smitten with tongues of two tartars,
I sat in my arm-chair and frowned
  Like one from the old book of martyrs ;
While lawyers played table the duck,
  With witnesses wary as partans,
Who joined in the game of pot luck—
  Their tempers as cross as clan tartans.

A cow had been lent out for hire,
  Her milk was to stand for her keeping,
But crummie grew tired of her byre,
  Of munching cold turnips, and sleeping ;
And so she got strangled past hope,
  But whether the rope the cow strangled,
Or whether she strangled the rope,
  Was ever the point that was mangled.

I wished that the beam and the string
  Had hung up the lawyers together,
Or ere it behoved them to swing
  My wits and their cow in one tether ;
I strove to make sense of their trash,
  Took snuff 'tween my nodding and yawning,
Till wink ! on black wings with a flash !
  I soared like a lark at the dawning.

The field it was green, and in hate
  Two lawyers poor crummie were haling
With tugs to a broken-down gate,
  And rugs to a gash in the railing ;
Till, whisk ! the pursuer went stot !
  And prod ! the defender fell screeching !
The one, with a tear in his coat,
  The other, a rent in his breeching.

At length, with the cow and the kink
  To settle, I made avizandum,
But fear, that with bullets of ink,
  My shots will be sadly at random ;—
Oh ! tempers of men are like chaff
  Which breath of two lawyers sets prinkling ;
When tossing a groat, with a laugh,
  Could end the dispute in a twinkling.

WINNING AND LOSING.

WHY ballad the glories of battle,
  And hymn the delights of the chase,
Nor sing of the rush and the rattle—
  The gallop that goes with a case?
When advocates storm the defences,
  And horsey-tails bounce at the bar ;
While peaceful pens, scoring expenses,
  Keep stroke with each cut and each scar.

Oh! hush thee! and hark to the story
  Of how, at the end of the day,
All covered with ink, and with glory,
  The winner retires from the fray!
The loser must finish his inning,
  Ere off from the field he can draw ;—
There's nought so delightful as winning,
  In all the delights of the law!

And yet, one would think, as at dinner,
  The hero would pay for the treat;
But no! for the foolish beginner
  Must pay for what caused his defeat!
His purse knows no picking or choosing,
  'Tis food for each ravenous maw ;—
There's nought so disgusting as losing,
  In all the disgusts of the law!

At chess, skittles, draughts, often gladly
  The game may be drawn with good grace ;
But, save when the reel's fankled sadly,
  There's no such resort in a case.
The Law's like the clock in Tron steeple,
  Whose weights gather weight as they run,
And ever this joy of the people,
  Keeps ticking the cost of the fun.

WHEN GOLDEN CROCUS CROWNS THE GREEN.

WHEN golden crocus crowns the green,
  The primrose at the wood's edge blows,
Tall daffodils in groups are seen
  Down where the river winding flows.
Ye flow'rs that in the sunshine burn,
  Ye cannot move him with your cheer,
Ye tell him but of spring's return,
  Ye say not that his love is near.

When redbreasts warble in the tree,
  And linnets sing within the wood,
The blackbird whistles, full and free,
  Far in the deeper solitude;
At dawn the skylark climbs the sky,
  At eve the thrush flings forth his note;
From north to south the grey clouds fly,
  From north to south his longings float.

The speckled thrush will cease erelong,
  The blackbird still his lay for joy;
Too full ! too full of love for song,
  When nesting-times their cares employ;
The crocus and the primrose then
  Will fade before the summer flow'rs —
His summer will be summer when
  His love returns to Scottish bow'rs.

ACCOMMODATION BILLS.

'TIS said, that in China,
  Grown men think it fine
To fly kites and dragons
  With plenty of twine ;
'Tis Briton's real earnest,
  This Chinaman's fun,
For hear how kite-flying
  In Britain is done :—

A. writes an acceptance
  For "value received,"—
'Tis false, but no matter,
  'Twill soon be believed, –
Gets *B.* to accept it,
  Confirming the lie,
The kite then in circle
  Is ready to fly.

A. quickly discounts it
  For money with *C.*,
Who passes it onward
  To *D.*, *E.*, *F.*, *G.*,
And everyone signs it,
  Nor thinks he has sinned,
And so it goes flying
  And raising the wind.

The string that sustains it,
　　As upward it strays,
Runs out, not by inches,
　　But measured by days,
And when these are ended.
　　At once, turvey top !
Upon the last holder
　　It falls with a drop.

Meanwhile *A.*, who made it,
　　Has lost the kite's price
Through some speculation
　　In rags, rum, or rice ;
And shows empty pockets,
　　With visage demure,
When asked to retire it
　　Grown old and mature.

Then, all who have signed it
　　With anger are riven,
To find that, "for value"
　　No value was given ;
But some one must pay it,
　　In wrath or goodwill,—
And that's the short tale of
　　A kite, or Wind Bill.

NEW YEAR'S SONG FOR COUNSEL.

COME, fling down the pencil and pen !
  Up chin with the bow and the fiddle !
We'll dance reels of eight and of ten,
  With hornpipes and jigs down the middle.
Oh ! who would be fighting in courts
  The weazands of cases to throttle,
When client to client resorts,
  First-footing with bun and with bottle ?

We'll deck out the Parliament Hall
  With misletoe bough and red berry,
With garlands of briefs on the wall
  'Mong evergreen arches so merry ;
Red tape from the statues will swing,
  With festoons of wigs from each rafter,
And all the long lobbies will ring
  With echoes of glorious laughter.

And then will be locked every door,
  And gowns o'er the windows hang pliant,
While dancing in groups on the floor
  Go bench and bar, agent and client,
Dundonnachie, facing Moncrieff,
  Will jig about flinging and flustered ;
While Nevay, with hooch of relief,
  Will kiss as he cleeks Betsy Mustard.

E

Our gowns will go fluttering when
    We waltz just like angels from Hades,
The senior boys being men,
    The junior choppers the ladies ;
Lord Advocate Balfour will dance
    With bearded Mackay for his lady,
While merry Macdonald will prance
    With Dickson hid under his plaidie.

We'll start Highland flings and jig mills,
    We'll toe the sword dance round a razor.
With Outer House Lords in quadrilles—
    M'Laren, Kinnear, Adam, Fraser ;
And then, just to make the reels go,
    We'll add till the figures run plainer,
Small alphabet Robertson's toe,
    Brand's heel and the sole of our Trayner.

With swinging of skirts fro and to,
    Each judge like a bobbing umbrella,
The red-robed divisions will do
    The fine country dance, Petronella ;
The President chassez and bow,
    The Justice-Clerk courtesy and answer,
And much-bewigged Shand, he will show
    Which Court can produce the best dancer.

Each dullard, good dancing who scorns,
  Each book-worm, and all the quill-pullers
Will blow up strathspeys on ink-horns,
  And finger out reels upon rulers.
Then criers, and clerks, and poor tools
  For once will be useful utensils,
And beat out the time on their stools
  And whistle up jigs upon pencils.

Then shut up my wig in my box,
  And banish my gown and my papers,
The New Year at every Court knocks,
  A truce to all vamping and vapours !
Here's luck to the client who knows
  What time to be gay as a feather !
Long life to the counsel who throws
  His cares and his gown off together !

SCOTCH HEATHER.

BRIGHT purple bloom of Scotland's hills,
Garb of her mountains, glens, and rills,
At sight of thee my bosom fills
   With memories proud
Of tartans, thistles, snuff, meal-mills,
   And mist-wet cloud.

Thy stem is like some fir-tree green
With twinkling bells hung thick between ;
Pressed to the earth, thou low dost lean,
   But scorns to break,
Up-springing quick as ne'er had been
   Foot on thy neck.

Thou'rt like the man when Fortune's tread
Falls fell and crushing on his head
Who bows, but when the blow has sped
   With dauntless will
He struggles up from sorrow's bed,
   A soldier still.

On storm-beat crags of dusky white
Where brackens wave their fans of light,
And rowans drop their berries bright
   The clefts between ;
Thy breast of purple on the height
   Is richly seen.

Home of the moor-cock, snipe, and deer,
The gaudy pheasant, crowing clear,
The partridge brown, that schemes her fear
   With draggled wings ;
And dappled grouse, when man draws near,
   That whirring springs.

Oft have I climbed the steep hill's side
'Mong hairsts of heather, deep and wide,
When sweet dust flew at every stride
   Like spendthrift's money,
And yellow bees could scarce abide
   The smell of honey.

On thee has patriot Wallace trod,
Who bled to break the tyrant's rod ;
And oft the Covenant's banner broad
   Has swept thy bloom,
Proclaiming at the pike's sharp shod
   Oppression's doom.

But why should thy small purple flower
Be dyed with blood in peaceful hour,
On moors, where men who creep and cower
   With guns resort,
To pour on birds a leaden show'r
   And call it sport?

When dogs and guns are laid to sleep,
'Neath the cleft moon thy sweet bells weep
To hear the plaintive dying peep
      From birds half killed,
As, from soft breasts, sore wounded deep,
      Their life's distilled.

No more the dusky legs will spring,
No more will spread the speckled wing;
A bloody head does earthward hing
      No more to live.—
'Tis sport to some to take the thing
      They cannot give.

Badge of true manhood and the brave,
Long may thy purple glory wave
O'er moor and hill, when red guns rave,
      And death's abroad ;
To shield the weak thou can'st not save,
      Bright flower of God.

ON OATHS.

THERE is a little thing
    Which magistrates administer,
Said with the hand upraised,
    In their peculiar way;
The great judicial oath,
    With smiling face or sinister,
Told like a parrot rhyme
    For witnesses to say.

But surely it is plain,
    Amid the law's verbosity,
That if a man would lie
    Or falsify his soul.
'Tis not in swearing oaths,
    Or any such monstrosity,
To bind him to the truth,
    Or keep him conscience whole.

'Tis not the oath he fears,—
    'Twould take an act of surgery,
To get into some heads
    Its weight and meaning due,—
'Tis not the power of awe,
    But 'tis the dread of perjury,
That tooths the legal vice
    And turns the legal screw.

To ears both quick and slow,
  To willing tongues and stuttering,
The judge supplies the words
  He recollects so well,
While some rush on before,
  So glibly are they uttering
The sacredest of things
  That sages fear to tell.

And shepherds tell their flocks
  Of curses and profanity,
Of wicked words in streets
  That wicked people say,
While in a court they'd find
  A text for all humanity,
Of how a sacred name
  Is cheapened every day.

SUMMER IS COMING.

THE twinkling snowdrop, with her parted bell,
Hath rung her farewell music in the dell;
The saffron daffodils, on green stalk slim,
Have danced in rings beside the river's brim;
By the wood's edge, 'mong mosses bronzed and wet,
Hath bloom'd and died the sweet wild violet :
The crocus burned his golden lamp and fled,
As o'er green lawns the snowy daisies spread,
And now the yellow primrose, from deep bowers,
Blows a faint challenge to the summer flowers.

THE GAME LAWS.

THE goldfinch, bullfinch, merle, and thrush,
　The chaffinch, lark, and linnet,
With sweeter airs fill hedge and bush
　Than flow from flute or spinet;
And why should these unsheltered be,
　When birds of bigger inches
Are shielded by the law's decree
　When flying, just like finches?

The blackcock, snipe, and speckled grouse,
　The duck and long-tailed pheasant,
The partridge in his spotted blouse,
　The ptarmigan so pleasant,
Go by the name of birds of game,
　Which means, that at their leisure
They're left to breed, that they may bleed
　When suits a lordling's pleasure.

For he who shoots, because he must,
　When beef and bread have risen,
And wife and children lack a crust,
　Will find himself in prison;
While he who shoots because he may,
　With dogs and gillies sporting,
Still finds himself from day to day
　With lords and squires consorting.

But measured by some wider laws,
  There's no man will deny it,
Who at a bird his trigger draws
  Upon his pan to fry it,
Is nobler than the wretch who sits
  Behind a beater's mud-shed,
To blow a cloud of wings to bits
  And glory in the bloodshed.

There's murder in yon dusky wood!
  There's slaughter on the heather!
When keepers, out in angry mood,
  And poachers rush together.
The game laws! the game laws!
  They make a kind heart callous,
And bring leal men, from hill and glen,
  To feed our jails and gallows.

THE SCRIBE'S HOLIDAY.

WHEN dropping cords of tasselled gold
　The low laburnum spreads,
And snowy hawthorn's bending bough
　With fragrant lilac weds,
In rustic coat, with switching cane,
　Down lanes of leafy twigs,
I seek for wisdom more than dwells
　In hills of horse-hair wigs.

Then, woodlands wave their leafy locks,
　Then grassy fields are green,
And snowball clouds from palest blue,
　Roll shadows o'er the scene;
And when the grey-fringed curtains shake
　Their pearls on lakes and brooks,
I learn a lesson from the skies
　That is not writ in books.

When high the rainbow's humid arch
　Illumes the fading cloud,
And swift the skylark's pulsing wings
　Mount up with pipings loud,
The songster fills my dusty soul
　Full with such sweet reports,
They burst the stony walls from rooms,
　The gilded roofs from courts.

THE DYVOUR'S DRESS.

THOUGH our Bankruptcy Court
 Is so high and serene,
It has sometimes been called
 A white-washing machine;
Where a debtor goes in
 With his debts on his back,
And comes out a white sheep
 All discharged of his pack.

Now in matters of law,
 It is matter of fact,
That there's nothing so trite
 As an old Scottish Act;
And an old Scottish Act
 Has enacted and said—
That a man should be marked
 While his debts are unpaid.

Oh ! the magpie is black,
 And the magpie is white,
And that's how we know
 Little magpies by sight;
And the old Dyvour's Dress
 Marked as plainly the fellow,
For his one leg was black
 And the other was yellow.

Nor was that the whole garb,
  For his hat, coat, and vest
Were all made of like stuff,
  And like hue as the rest;
But that worthy old Act
  By an Act was' repealed,
And with whitewash and brass
  The old garb is concealed.

But at times, lawyers think,
  As they walk down the street,
Of some fine wealthy men,
  Whom they happen to meet:
" Oh ! go pay your old debts,
  You're a poor Dyvour fellow—
For your one leg is black,
  And the other still yellow."

STORNOWAY BAY.

THE sunset hath fled,
　With its saffron and crimson,
And clouds of dark purple
　Shut out the last ray;
The moon from her bed,
　Hath arisen o'er the mountains,
To dance on the waters
　Of Stornoway Bay.

Swept swiftly along,
　Glides the bark of the fisher,
And dark spreads his canvas
　Across the moon's way,
While faintly in song
　Comes the voice of his sweetheart,
Borne out from the headland
　Of Stornoway Bay.

Red-fringed are the shrouds
　That encurtain the sunset,
And golden the banners
　That herald the day;
But fairer than clouds,
　And to Ronald, thrice dearer,
Is witching young Bessie
　Of Stornoway Bay.

Her brow is as fair
   As the breast of the seagull,
Her cheeks are as lovely
   As roses in May,
Dark, dark is her hair
   As the skirt of the tempest—
The pride and the darling
   Of Stornoway Bay.

WHEN FIRST MY WIG WAS NEW.

WHEN first my horse-hair wig
  Looked out upon the world,
'Twas small, and white, and trig,
  And curled, and curled, and curled,
With wee curls on the crown,
  With side curls growing bolder,
While tail curls two hung down,
  And danced upon my shoulder.

In Court, when I stood up,
  I trow but I was saucy,
As proud as any pup,
  As pleased as any lassie;
I marked my sleeve's wide ring,
  My gown's deep-flowing vesture,
And thought how fine they'd swing,
  With every coming gesture.

I opened out my case
  In half a recitation,
And then, I lost my place,
  O'er some small variation;
While racked with mental wrench—
  " What is the point you're making? "
Came sneering from the Bench,
  And set my knees a-quaking.

F

I strove to find my thread—
   'Twas like a thread of spider,
Up-fankled in my head—
   And still the breach grew wider.
A pot-lid seemed my wig!
   My gown, a steaming blanket;—
I danced a humble jig
   Ere from that bar I shankit!

But now my wig is brown,
   My gown is all in tatters,
And when my thread has flown,
   I never heed who chatters;
But thrash out word on word,
   Like sportsman in the heather;
For if you lose one bird,
   Good whacks will start another.

THE SCOTTISH BLACKBIRD.

WITHDRAWN a furlong from the sea's white marge
  Stands Rosneath's avenue of centuried yews ;
An old-world street, roofed green with branches
    large,
Home of the squirrel, glossed with tearful dews.

Betwixt red sundown and the blue of night,
  At gloaming's tender hour, with footstep slow
I sought this path, to mark the fading light,
  And feel in thought the day's sweet afterglow.

'Twas in this grove I heard the blackbird sing,—
  Prophetic were his raptures, loud his lay ;
Whistling of summer in the steps of spring,
  Singing of sunshine at the close of day.

In full, flute tones from upraised rippling-throat,
  The coal-black singer of the crocus bill,
Across Clyde's listening Gareloch flung his note,
  That woke the slumbering echoes of each hill.

From budding elms outflanked in double line
  Small birds rang chorus through the green
    domain,
Till in rich voice, with modulation fine,
  The wizard's solo drowned the choir again.

And at each pause, my waiting, beating heart
   Told o'er his notes in echoed rhythmic throng,
Thrilled with the singer's masterhood of art—
   As eloquent in pauses as in song.

At sleep's still hour, when shook the evening star,
   I heard him, hastened by the moon's soft ray,
Calling farewell, to brothers known afar,
   As to the woods he winged his rapid way.

For song's repose, how fitting is this place !
   When vesper singers to their nests have flown,
Where mournful yews their plumage interlace,
   And meditation treads the path alone.

THE SUMMER VACATION.

HURRAH ! for the Session is done,
   The battle of cases is over,
The holiday season's begun,
   The advocate now is a rover;
Oh ! pity the Lord on the Bills,
   In town in this glorious weather,
While we to the lochs and the hills
   Go off to green fern and red heather.

We scatter like boys full of jokes
   As out of the school they go roaming,
Too soon to return, full of croaks,
   Like crows in the trees at the gloaming ;
But he who would name the word "case,"
   On holiday tour or procession,
A palm on the nose of his face
   Should rub out the foolish expression.

Tweed coated, 'neath whispering trees,
   With fishing-rod, airy and pliant,
Far drawn from refreshers and fees,
   Deep hid from clerk, W.S., or client,
I'll think of yon tenantless courts,
   With doors, some to Heav'n, some to Hades,
Where never a footstep resorts,
   Except of the tourists or ladies.

No longer with reading of prints
    Our brains will go round in our craniums,
Or tugging of gowns and broad hints
    Will make us as hot as geraniums ;
Dropt down in some deep Highland glen,
    With idleness for occupation,
At rest and at peace with all men,
    I'll dream out my summer vacation.

BURN FISHING.

Go bring to me my rod and reel,
   That I may thrash the running water,
What though I catchna trout or eel!
   Creel toom or fu' it doesna matter!
I'll pass the day wi' loup and splatter
   Frae stane to stane, the linns among,
And think, how different is the chatter
   Of brattling stream to lawyer's tongue.

Beneath the hazels blinks the burn,
   A sparkling path of brown disorder,
Through mossy stanes and dripping fern,
   Banked in wi' heather's purple border;
Where, tacket shod, the careless forder,
   Forth splashes wi' his dangling gut,
Without a fear of Court recorder,
   To note his seeming want o' wut.

When, whisking through the leafy trees.
   I cast my flies of grey and yellow,
On mirror pools, whereon the breeze
   Writes dimpling smiles of ridge and hollow;
I'll think whiles on the logic mellow,
   With which we try the Judge to catch,   .
When, if ae cast should miss the fellow,
   Another throw may be his match.

My reel, my rod of ash feet ten,
  My basket, casts, and book of hooks,
Awhile thou'lt be my supple pen,
  And thou shalt be my book of books :
I'll watch but how the burnie jouks
  Where troutlets leap and linties sing,
And e'en forget my legal looks
  In whipping water wi' a string.

Let hunters charge the five-barred gate,
  Let racers bet away their treasure,
Let sportsmen pour their blast of hate,
  And tramps, tramp out their month of leisure,
There's nothing gives such gentle pleasure,
  To lawyer, sawyer, churl, or duke,
As paidlin', daidlin' in a measure,
  About a burnie wi' a hook.